Empath The Book

Empath The Book

Over 500 Aphorisms and Secrets about Empaths

TheFallBackUp

© 2021 by Christopher Dwayne
TheFallBackUp

Empath the Book

Self-Published
introvertempath@gmail.com
www.themeditationfamily.com
www.patreon.com/themeditationfamily

ISBN: 9798756308938

Empath The Book

Welcome to *Empath the Book*. This book contains over 500 aphorisms about Empaths.

An Empath is a person that can feel, sense, and alter the emotions and energies of other people. This book is written by an Empath about Empaths from an Empath's point of view.

Enjoy this book and don't forget to pledge to our wellness center fund by going to www.patreon.com/hemeditationfamily to help us create more books, videos and wellness centers for the community.

Introduction

Empaths are beings who feel deeply and heal others by feeling the feelings of others. This book will go through over 500 quick aphorisms facts secrets and realizations about Empaths by the mystic Christopher 'TheFallBackUp' Dwayne. This book will not go deep into the science of Empaths as a study of psychology or definitive science from a scientist point of view but instead will give mini thoughts known as aphorisms or sutras about Empaths. These aphorisms are the realizations about Empaths as they came to the author in meditation. Think of this as a guide for Empaths by an Empath, or a guide for those who seek to learn a deeper meaning to what Empaths are by an Empath. This guide is made to help you find a deeper perspective about Empaths past the normal psychology point of view. Enjoy!

Empath Sutras

1. Empaths are on Earth to heal the negative mindset of humanity, in terms of its relationship with the Earth and its life force energy

2. Empaths feel your emotions even if they don't know you

Empaths The Book

3. Empaths fall in love with loving people

4. Empaths attract people who need healing

5. Empaths heal themselves by healing others

6. Empaths need time in nature to ground after taking on too much energy

7. Empaths will retreat to solitude if their energy is disturbed too much in a social setting

8. Empaths are pulled into their life path by following the energy of the universe

9. Empaths do better when they attune themselves to the energies of the universe through energy therapy

10. Yes, Empaths are a real thing

11. Everyone is an Empath by nature but many don't nurture it or treat their energies as sacred so they suffer from it in life unknowingly

12. Empaths need rest like introverts need to recharge

13. Empaths need time to introvert at times in order to recharge

14. Empaths are creatives

15. Empaths use creativity to express and release their emotions

16. Empaths can feel the energy of the people on their social media

17. Empaths who listen to their gut win at life

18. Empaths who move off of their passion in life and listen to their gut win at life

19. Empaths have the best gut feelings, also known as instinct or connection to spirit guides.

20. Empaths receive messages from a divine source through their gut instincts

21. Empaths listen to their gut; when they don't they suffer

Empaths The Book

22. Empaths who follow their spiritual path win at life

23. Empaths have existed for all of human history

24. All religious figures were renowned Empaths as they felt the pain and love of the people and sought to heal them

25. Empaths are good friends

26. Empaths have deep love for their true friends and seek to help their friends be better people

27. Empaths may guide you to miracles through their instincts

Empaths The Book

28. Not all Empaths believe they are Empaths but they are Empaths if their feelings guide them

29. Empaths can have up and down emotions if they do not release energy

30. Empaths emotions are governed by the movements and phases of the moon so Empaths who follow the moon's phases win at life

31. Empaths need friends who give good vibes

32. Empaths become their friends

33. Empaths who do not know they are Healers suffer

34. Empaths who chase their dreams in life usually succeed because of their divine intuition

Empaths The Book

35. Empaths love deeply

36. Empaths need long periods of time alone to get over broken hearts

37. Empaths are great relationship partners because of their deep emotional bonds

38. Empaths who train can feel your pain by touching you and can move it out of your body

39. Empathic Touch is a technique created by the author of this book that uses intuitive touch, sound frequencies, crystals, and Talk Yoga to promote a positive flow in the body to improve the immune system

40. Empathic healing is not accepted as a mainstream form of healing since it would disprove a lot of lies that are told to humanity through the allopathic medical associations throughout history

41. Empaths can become energetically drained from being in uncomfortable situations

42. Empaths make bad decisions when they are mad and frustrated

43. Empaths who take time to relax when they are frustrated win at life since many of their emotions are given to them

44. Empaths feel their way in and out of situations

45. Empaths are your guardian angels in real life since they seek to make you feel better about yourself and your life before they depart from your space

Empaths The Book

46. Empaths can be great healers if they work on their skills

47. Empaths release a lot of emotions by listening to or making music and being creative

48. Empaths who are in tune with the Earth's energies win at life

49. Empaths are not always born; sometimes life occurrences, like traumas or simple realizations, turn people into Empaths

50. Empaths can be hyper-sensitive at times

51. Empaths who eat mostly vegan foods enhance their abilities by eliminating the energies of dead flesh

Empaths The Book

52. Empaths in ancient times were given high regard in society and even leadership roles as oracles or seers

53. Empaths forgive. If you are an Empath, forgiving clears your energy highways and makes you a better conduit for subtle energies to flow

54. Empaths who learn their Chakras and take care of them enhance their abilities

55. Being an Empath is really supposed to be a major part of human evolution but this is being blocked so that society is easier to control

56. The increase in Empaths is a direct result of the Earth's base resonance frequency increasing within the past couple of decades

Empaths The Book

57. Empaths who are in tune with their ancestors have enhanced abilities in the now

58. Empaths can feel their ancestors when their spirits are close and this gives them power and motivation to do great things

59. Empaths feel spirits so your words don't mean too much to them since they know the intention of your heart

60. Empaths can fall in love with emotional people easily since they love to emotional heal people

61. Empaths can cure diseases with their presence

62. Empaths are the cure to many emotional, spiritual, and frequency imbalances

Empaths The Book

63. Empaths often go into fields of energy healing such as therapy, yoga instructors, reiki practitioners and community organizing

64. Empaths are the creatives you want on your team. If you find a good Empath that knows them-self, keep them around

65. Empaths are often taken advantage of because of the knowledge of the previous fact

66. Empaths notice double numbers, triple numbers, and number sequences period. It's the Universe talking to them and guiding them

67. Empaths who do yoga win at life

68. Empaths who wear sandals or no shoes at all win at life since energy is released back into the Earth through the feet and Empaths need to keep energy flowing

Empaths The Book

69. Empaths feel the good vibes coming off of these words

70. Empaths come in many levels, there are those who feel a little and there are those who feel a lot. There is no bar set to be an Empath

71. Empaths feel the issues of people we have never met on TV and on social media feeds

72. Empaths are great detectives

73. Empaths see what you don't because they see things with their intuition and not just their eyes

74. Empaths who incorporate crystals into their daily life enhance their abilities

75. Empaths feel what's coming

Empaths The Book

76. Empaths may speak the future without realizing it and realize it later once what they said occurs

77. Empaths think ahead because they feel ahead

78. Empaths may have to cancel plans due to unexpected changes in the way they feel about the energy

79. Empaths have clear dreams that tell of future events

80. Empaths try to avoid dramatic people and situations when they detect bad vibes and energy

81. Empaths who are in homes where they have no space or personal privacy feel smothered and seek to live a free life with time for themselves

82. Empaths are introverts when dealing with up and down emotions but can be quite extroverted when doing things they love

83. Empaths are motivated by love

84. Empaths feel what you're not telling them

85. Empaths don't like when you hold back emotions from them

86. Empaths are truth advocates

87. Empaths have a divine connection with nature

88. Empaths motivate their friends to be as happy as they can

Empaths The Book

89. Empaths are joy advocates

90. Empaths who listen to the signs the universe is sending them win at life

91. Empath's gut feelings are really the universe and their ancestors speaking through them

92. Empaths will tell you the truth about what they feel is the best thing for you

93. Empaths can be any age

94. Empaths make great psychic mediums

95. Empaths make great artist and poets

96. Empaths have divine ideas that come from their divine intuition

Empaths The Book

97. Empaths make the best out of all situations to heal the situation from low vibrations

98. Empaths don't agree with negative or pessimistic thinking

99. Empaths feel emotional pain physically, that's why they don't like you to feel bad

100. Empaths who find a good daily routine win at life

101. Empaths are as peaceful as possible to avoid bad vibes

102. Empaths give great guidance

103. Empath's guidance is accurate and can help you to avoid being in a situation that is bad for you

104. Empaths will keep trying until they succeed at making the vibes good again

Empaths The Book

105. Empaths love with purpose so if you love an Empath, love with purpose

106. Empath's existence heals others

107. Empaths who work together can make very miraculous events occur

108. Empaths feel the things that need to be done before they realize why they are feeling them

109. Empaths listen to their inner voice even when it seems crazy to everyone else

110. Empaths root for the underdog

Empaths The Book

111. Empaths know when they see a sign from the universe that's made for them and will tell you even if you don't believe them

112. Empaths try to keep certain people around them that they feel will give them a good mood

113. Empaths often try to run from their destiny as healers and spiritual guides

114. Empaths can feel depressed and use drugs to overcome their up and down feeling, but this is not good for them and does not stop the effects of being an Empath

115. Empaths are needed to balance the universal energies of the world

116. Empaths turn their partners into Empaths as well just by being energetically connected with them for long periods of time

Empaths The Book

117. Empaths can use their gifts to help others or for their personal use

118. Empaths make great healers

119. Empaths can use their healing abilities as a great career such as counseling or therapy

120. Empaths make great motivational speakers

121. Empaths feel what's not being said

122. Empaths move when the universe wants it to happen

123. Empaths feel you looking at them, even at long distances

124. Empaths are often frustrated by their own abilities

Empaths The Book

125. Empaths are creeped out by people with no feelings

126. Empaths who help the Earth win at life

127. Empaths can end up being very spiritual or religious people later in life

128. Empaths are charged by real love

129. Empaths are drained by fake love

130. Empaths become the complaint box for their friends and family

131. Empaths who are benevolent win at life since their true nature is to be benevolent beings

132. Empaths are extremely intuitive

Empaths The Book

133. Empaths were not accepted by the medical associations because science could not explain intuition. As Carl Jung put it "When a man has a hunch we do not know where that hunch comes from"

134. Empaths are connected to a divine source of information that many believe to be the Akashic Records of the Universe

135. Empaths are the ones people call when they need help

136. Empaths find ways to make the impossible happen in order to bring peace back to their life

137. Empath's inner peace is important to them

Empaths The Book

138. Empaths make great business people as they can feel the trends of change that make a good entrepreneur successful

139. Empaths sense danger so if you see one running away from something unknown...run

140. Empath's dreams can say a lot about the energies they take in

141. Empaths who have children together create very gifted children

142. Empaths are often concerned about the future of the world and humanity

143. Empaths don't like war but will fight one for peace

144. Empaths tell the truth to not waste time and opportunity

Empaths The Book

145. Empaths should take their own advice more. They give great advice but to often try not to think about the things they need to hear themselves

146. Empaths heal with words so they often play mediator in conflicts

147. Empaths can take on the personality of others if around them for too long

148. Empaths will go to extremes to heal

149. Empaths like feeling as free as possible

150. Empaths will end friendships with people they feel don't want to evolve

151. Empaths are often very wise about life decisions, even when their decisions sound crazy to others

Empaths The Book

152. Empaths who use crystals to heal themselves of stagnant energies win at life

153. Empaths will do things they don't want to if you ask them for help

154. Empaths use art to give a visual or vibrational representation of their inner emotions and subtle energies

155. Empaths escape using music

156. Empaths need solitude to recharge just like introverts

157. Empaths follow their hearts

158. Empaths want everyone to get along and will find a way to make it so everyone has a reason to

Empaths The Book

159. Empaths see repeating numbers when they start to follow their life path destiny of helping others

160. Empaths make great leaders since they can feel the direction in which they must lead everyone

161. Empaths who sun gaze during sunrise and sunset enhance their abilities

162. Empath's stomachs are sensitive to energy since the stomach is the brain of the spiritual body

163. Empaths attract miracles to themselves that can be seen and observed by others

164. Empaths seek a life of love peace and bliss but are forced to overcome obstacles in order to have that in their own life

Empaths The Book

165. Empath's life path number greatly influence their day to day life

166. Empath's eating habits, which can be different for each Empath, affect their emotional life

167. Empaths are sensitive to the universe around them and can even feel shifts in planets and star alignments in their own personal lives

168. Empaths are greatly affected by the transitions of the zodiac constellations

169. Empaths love making love; the act of being with another sensually is a sacred act to an Empath

170. Empaths often judge themselves too much

Empaths The Book

171. Empaths can get stuck in their emotions

172. Empaths can have mood swings if around too many different types of emotional people

173. Empaths get messages from the universe telling them what to do next

174. Empaths are hero types

175. Empaths can feel your emotional state over the phone

176. Empaths who write down how they feel win at life

177. Empaths can read your mind through the change in your mood, voice, and facial expressions

Empaths The Book

178. Empaths have been targeted by government agencies in top secret programs that wanted to make them super soldiers and weapons

179. Empaths will match your intensity if you try to argue with one

180. Empaths triple your love and give it back to you if you decide to love one

181. Empaths love music that speaks about the situations they are going through

182. Empaths are good friends; not always there when you want, but here when you need

183. Empaths put their family and children before anything else

Empaths The Book

184. Empaths don't always like to be Empaths since it's a lot of dealing with energies and emotions

185. Empaths seek to create their own reality but often get swept up in the reality of others

186. Empaths who love their abilities win at life

187. Empaths can feel weather shifts coming with enough accuracy to avoid disasters

188. Empaths can feel emotional changes in the atmosphere around them

189. Empaths feel what you need, you just have to let them

190. Empaths should learn to say "no" without feeling bad or they will be used by many people

Empaths The Book

191. Empaths keep their mind on things that bring peace and love to their life

192. Empaths can have weird personalities at times as they deal with the emotions of others

193. Empaths are very creative and use creativity as an escape

194. Empaths feel the pain of people far away

195. Empaths are not always born that way and can be more empathic or less empathic at different times in their life

196. Empaths can be very emotional; know this before dating one so you remember to be nurturing instead of complaining
Empaths The Book

197. Empaths are not just human; there are animals with this ability as well like the cat, the dog, the goat, and the owl

198. Empaths make great actors and actresses since they express emotions well

199. Empaths heal their family traumas by changing patterns within themselves that cause them trauma

200. Empaths learn from their miracles

201. Empaths can be introverted around family growing up

202. Empaths who use chant mantras enhance their abilities, heal themselves, and win at life

203. Empaths hold onto good memories to relive them later during times when bad memories are being made

Empaths The Book

204. Empaths feel the energy of the universe so they make great reiki and empathic touch practitioners

205. Empaths live legendary lives once they take their abilities seriously

206. Empaths who are in tune with nature win at life

207. Empaths are called to nature

208. Empaths love a date in nature

209. Empaths and waterfalls just get along so well

210. Empaths who learn meditation and take it serious win at life

Empaths The Book

211. Empaths who learn about the third eye win at life

212. Empaths are usually the last to talk in the conversation

213. Empaths stress you out when they are stressed in order to ease stress on themselves

214. Empaths who take walks balance their energies and win at life

215. Empaths write great stories and have vivid imaginations

216. Empaths stop what they are doing to help others

217. Empaths are the person helping the old lady walk across the street

Empaths The Book

218. Empaths know that peace and love make the world a good place to live in

219. Empaths who know that love comes from us not to us are better at being Empaths and therefore win at life

220. Empaths make good plans that change their life instead of just allowing fate to take over

221. Empaths feel the future coming

222. Empaths feel your moods and it makes them moody or less moody depending on how moody you are

223. Empaths who practice martial arts have better energy control and therefore win at life

224. Empaths love to feel comfortable

Empaths The Book

225. Empaths who feel comfortable experience inner bliss and this occurrence heals others around them

226. Empath leaders are more diplomatic and less aggressive

227. Empaths listen to their heart over their brain

228. Empaths who date see miracles together

229. Empaths feel the tether of other people's emotions

230. Empaths who learn how to sever spirit ties when needed win at life

231. Empaths don't need long conversations to know how you feel

Empaths The Book

232. Empaths are loving people who seek love as often as possible

233. Empaths who master the power of the smile win at life

234. Empaths catch feelings easily

235. Empaths take on the traits of their parents but seek to fix the spiritual dilemmas their parents suffered from

236. Empaths hold a lot in, without telling people, to protect themselves and others from uncertain feelings

237. Empaths feel sleepy when the people around them start to feel sleepy

238. Empaths are bad vibe furnaces using their own vessel to dissipate the bad vibes in others

Empaths The Book

239. Empaths can feel your childhood traumas

240. Empaths like socializing but love being alone relaxing

241. Empaths live according to the mood

242. Empaths will walk on eggshells to avoid conflict

243. Empaths, even if prepared for battle, will opt for peace in a situation to avoid draining energy

244. Empaths who have Empath friends win at life

245. Empaths who keep their spaces sacred are better prepared for healing and therefore win at life

Empaths The Book

246. Empaths are lovers and fighters and all other emotions in between

247. Empaths who can stay focused even when emotional win at life

248. Empaths will accept your invitation then not show up to save themselves from awkward energy

249. Empaths like to talk about feelings

250. Empaths have close bonds with their pets

251. Empaths love love more than anything else; even careers and goals become based around the desires of the heart

252. Empaths are great listeners

253. Empaths listen to the things not being said

Empaths The Book

254. Empaths feel the emotional temperament of crowds

255. Empaths who grow gardens are better at controlling their energies and therefore win at life

256. Empaths won't go places where there are bad vibes

257. Empaths love good guidance

258. Empaths who educate themselves about being an Empath win at life

259. Empaths are nature's way of keeping humans emotionally in check

260. Empaths who date hurt people, often heal them and help them to become emotionally balanced

Empaths The Book

261. Empaths can sense when something important is about to happen

262. Empaths should be mindful of what they say because they tend to speak things into existence

263. Empaths can predict future events with their intuition

264. Empaths know when you're telling the truth or when you're thinking something else

265. Empaths can have quick tempers if always around emotionally unstable people

266. Empaths just need peace to heal

267. Empaths feel their way into and out of situations

Empaths The Book

268. Empaths who experience trauma at a young age seek to correct these things in the world later on in life

269. Empaths love to make love...and peace

270. Empaths will show you so much love when they have a crush on you

271. Empaths hear and see signs from the universe in nature, in numbers, and in random conversations

272. Empaths who use their abilities to foreshadow things before they happen to avoid bad situations or take advantage of good situations win at life

273. Empaths should be as honest as possible because karma works fast for Empaths

Empaths The Book

274. Empaths who feel like they want something enough manifest that thing or something like that thing pretty fast

275. Empaths live for love

276. Empaths want everyone to win at life

277. Empaths love cute adorable things

278. Empaths don't like aggressive politicians

279. Empaths feel the best when in their comfort zones

280. Empaths can get stuck in their comfort zones so Empaths who take risks to get farther in life win at life

281. Empath's dreams contain important signs and messages for the Empath and others

Empaths The Book

282. Empaths who meditate receive great ideas and epiphanies

283. Empaths can unconsciously take on the emotions of another and not be sure exactly who they received the emotions from

284. Empaths can become depressed when they are lacking love

285. Empaths do better around people who are sensitive to their emotions

286. Empaths have visions of their own future

287. Empaths have a gift but don't always see it as a gift

288. Empaths should purposely avoid bad energy

289. Empaths should purposely emit good energy

290. Empaths need time away from people to recharge

291. Empaths who use grounding techniques win at life

292. Empaths hope you do well

293. Empaths are ultimately seeking to heal themselves by healing others

294. Empaths who seek to help you, let them

295. Empaths feel the flow of a situation and know when to keep going and when not to

Empaths The Book

296. Empaths who use their abilities to help themselves save a lot of wasted energy and win at life

297. Empaths can feel when someone likes them

298. Empaths are attracted to positive energy

299. Empaths will disappear if the vibe is off

300. Empaths who listen to their own intuition win at life

301. Empaths can be emotionally sensitive

302. Empaths can be introverted but not all Empaths are introverts

303. Empaths are affected by changes in nature

Empaths The Book

304. Empaths try to avoid obstacles before they come

305. Empaths will help guide you back to love and peace in your life

306. Empaths who don't rush win at life

307. Empaths can feel it in their spirit when someone is genuinely good or bad

308. Empaths who listen before speaking win at life

309. Empaths feel when people change their mind

310. Empaths have had to hide their abilities in the past to not be labeled evil by societies of the past

Empaths The Book

311. Empaths who speak with love win at life

312. Empaths are all over the world, in every race, in every tribe

313. Empaths will go far to make sure the love of their life loves them back

314. Empaths are great students; they feel the real meaning and origins behind words

315. Empaths feel better about their life when everyone is happy around them

316. Empaths often get sucked into situations that have nothing to do with them

317. Empaths are moved by the flow of the moon and sun's energies on the Earth

318. Empaths who learn to control their temper win at life

319. Empaths can become shy and emotionally distant if around to many bad vibes

320. Empaths who find time for vacations in nature, or better yet, a life in nature, win at life

321. Empaths who master feeling the emotions of others without taking on the energy of others win at life

322. Empaths have quick karma so it's best they become benevolent being instead of unrighteous individuals

323. Empaths fit in with any crowd giving them a chameleon like personality

Empaths The Book

324. Empaths follow the voice in their head and the feeling in their heart but need to learn how to take a step back before making decisions purely off of emotions for best results

325. Empaths feel the truth

326. Empaths can get in the habit of staying up late releasing emotions

327. Empaths who face their fears win at life

328. Empaths feel when close friends and family are in trouble

329. Empaths get the greatest ideas from the universe

330. Empaths get anxiety due to overthinking about the future so Empaths who learn to live in the moment win at life

Empaths The Book

331. Empaths who focus on completing tasks without being distracted by emotions or stray thoughts win at life

332. Empaths pick up on songs playing on the radio when they are not listening to the radio and sing them out loud

333. Empaths pick up on the change in emotions in friends and family

334. Empaths keep to themselves when they first realize they are Empaths

335. Empaths use their spirit to get through things

336. Empaths are fearless once they find themselves and become comfortable with it

337. Empaths feel anxiety physically

Empaths The Book

338. Empaths get physically sick being around bad vibes

339. Empaths will leave a job if they feel pressured or uncomfortable with the energies at the job

340. Empaths don't know they are Empaths most of the time and it takes for them to read books like this or watch videos to realize what they are

341. Empaths who seek to help other people win at life

342. Empaths are caring people and genuinely want to help you succeed but they need you to believe in yourself so they can do their job

343. Empaths feel the vibe of their environment

Empaths The Book

344. Empaths feel the vibe change so they can expect things before they happen

345. Empaths retreat to reorganize, release, recharge, and regroup before coming back out

346. Empaths know when there is something going on that is not being said

347. Empaths who feel confident in their abilities win at life

348. Every mother is an Empath

349. Every newborn is an Empath

350. Everyone who feels empathy is not an Empath; everyone can feel empathy but not everyone has heightened intuition because of it

351. Empaths treat every situation with feeling

Empaths The Book

352. Empaths who write books win at life

353. Empaths who put as much time into their dreams as they do other people's dreams win at life

354. Empaths who have a spiritual routine win at life

355. Empaths should meditate as much as possible to gain the ability to release and manipulate the energies around them

356. Empaths are often gifted painters musicians and creatives

357. Empaths deal with a lot of emotions, mostly those of other people
Empaths The Book

358. Empaths who keep a happy thought to go back to win at life

359. Empaths who learn about herbs, all types, and their properties win at life

360. Empaths who treat people kind win at life

361. Empaths are more in tune with animals since most animals on Earth are empathic

362. Empaths are pet people

363. Empaths are pro love

364. Empaths are motivational people when they finally get to know themselves and their abilities

365. Empaths are in your family… guaranteed

Empaths The Book

366. Empaths have abilities they can train and make better like healing with touch, voice, and presence

367. Empaths can become very introverted or extroverted over time depending on their experiences as an Empath growing up and in a career

368. Empaths are great leaders

369. Empaths are great interviewers since they are sincerely good listeners and care what you're saying

370. Empaths are not around things for too long that do not keep them with some type of joy or love

371. Empaths can feel who the negative person is in the room

Empaths The Book

372. Empaths can feel who the positive people are in the room

373. Empaths start their day seeking to make things better

374. Empaths make the best out of every situation

375. Empaths feel the attention being put on them

376. Empaths know when you change your mind from far distances

377. Empaths who deal with their emotions and don't hold them in win at life

Empaths The Book

378. Empaths follow their life path without knowing it, as the energy of life pulls them into the situations they are predestined to be in

379. Empaths who learn to love learning win at life

380. Empaths know how you feel right now if they are in the room with you. Try it; look around the room and in your head tell yourself how each person feels then ask them to see how accurate you are

381. Empaths love as a way of life

382. Being an Empath is something you feel

383. Empaths will start things and not complete them if their spirit tell them to

384. Empaths are spirit led individuals

Empaths The Book

385. Empaths just know…and if you don't know what that means…ask an Empath

386. Empaths give intuitive advice so listen to the messages behind the message for best results

387. Empaths feel the things that go without saying

388. Empaths love knowing the history of things and where things come from so they may know the real energy of things

389. Empaths ask a lot of questions if they feel something is the matter

390. Empaths need to feel understood

391. Empaths love to fully understand

Empaths The Book

392. Empaths attract the love they want to themselves by being the energy they want to attract

393. Empaths who realize they are attracting the emotions and energies around them will adjust their own energies to attract better energies

394. Empaths should connect more with one another to better understand themselves as individuals

395. Empath's touch can make you feel calm, loving, and more blissful

396. Empaths, be mindful of the media you watch and listen to, as your moods can be easily manipulated by the information and energy resonance of the media you consume

Empaths The Book

397. Empaths who are children should be allowed to practice and grow their abilities so they have more productive lives

398. Empaths love using their imagination

399. Empaths are great at predicting future events

400. Empaths are great at predicting the outcome of stories or conversations

401. Empaths were studied by Carl Jung who was one of the first people to diagnose introverts and extroverts

402. Empaths feel the vibe of the day when they wake up

Empaths The Book

403. Empaths seek a much more peaceful and free world

404. Empaths will change the future of humanity and how humanity develops moving forward

405. Empaths are great futurists

406. Empaths want to see their family do great in life, even if they don't say it or express it all the time

407. Empaths are really focused people when they need to be

408. Empaths who plan "Me" days... win at life

409. Empath's feelings are sacred to them

410. Empaths sense your true intentions

Empaths The Book

411. Empaths don't always want to help people but are compelled to by their spirit

412. Empaths don't like to be associated with bad vibes

413. Empaths don't like to associate with people with bad vibes

414. Empaths who associate with people with bad vibes end up giving other people bad vibes later

415. Empaths become the top 3 people they know and hang around with

416. Empaths are always looking for new ways to express their inner selves

417. Empaths avoid bad situations by listening to their gut

Empaths The Book

418. Empaths know when they are looking at a sign from the universe that is for them

419. Empaths should seek to not eat meats since the meats contain the emotional signature of the animal that was killed

420. Empaths can not explain everything that happens around them and don't seek to because they feel others won't understand or believe them

421. Empaths who find a good routine win at life

422. Empaths unconsciously seek a blissful existence

423. Empaths feel that they need to help people who they don't necessarily need to be helping

Empaths The Book

424. Empaths never give up on love

425. Empaths need time after taking on the energies of others to release those energies and recharge through solitude

426. Empaths are introverts who feel

427. Empaths are extroverts who make changes in their community

428. Empaths are all about working together to accomplish the goal

429. Empaths can make bad decisions due to their unchecked emotions and feelings

430. Empaths need time to recharge

431. Empaths enjoy time in bed

Empaths The Book

432. Empaths enjoy relaxation

433. Empaths love a good movie and feel for the characters

434. Empaths seek to have balanced families but will retreat from family if they feel misunderstood

435. Empaths will go through pain if it gets them to their ultimate goal of peace

436. Empaths who don't join specific groups win at life

437. Empath's intuition is very accurate and should be listened to

438. Empaths make decisions off of their feelings and intuition that others cannot feel and therefore are not always understood

Empaths The Book

439. Empaths are driven by destiny

440. It's important for Empaths to know what they want in life or they will attract things they don't like

441. It's important for Empaths to express their true feelings to people

442. It's important for Empaths to feel they tried their best to help you

443. Empaths who wear no clothes win at life since Empaths release energy through their epidermis

444. Empaths feel the energy in repeating numbers

445. Empaths get anxiety when they are close to a breakthrough

Empaths The Book

446. Empaths feel the energy of the past heavily during retrogrades

447. Empaths are heavily influenced by the moon

448. Empaths who cannot stand up for themselves get dragged into things they don't want to do

449. Empaths who learn when to say "yes" or "no" win at life

450. Empaths…go for your dreams in life…you will catch them

451. Empaths can feel their calling in life

452. Empaths can take on and become the energy of the music they listen to

Empaths The Book

453. Empaths can detox from music by not listening to music with words for 30 days

454. Empaths can get over anxiety by reminding themselves the future and past can only exist as a thought and the right now moment is all there will ever be

455. Empaths who learn about sound resonance and frequency healing win at life and live a better more attuned life

456. Empaths see patterns

457. Empaths see and heal family curses

458. Empaths love the endless beauty of nature

459. Empaths who travel win at life

Empaths The Book

460. Empaths who find their love match win at life

461. Empaths who find the love within themselves and love themselves so much that they don't need love from outside of themselves win at life

462. Empaths are normal people and it is normal to be an Empath

463. Empaths are more or less sensitive to the energies of others at different times in their life depending on life circumstances

464. Empaths listen to bad advice and then do the right thing anyways

465. Empaths who face their fears win at life

Empaths The Book

466. Empaths can get caught up in the building of others' empires

467. Empaths take on the personality of others if they are around them for too long

468. Empaths can feel when they are not wanted in a place

469. Empaths love to feel at home

470. Empath's home is where their heart is

471. Empaths share the most traits with introverts

472. Empaths are great in relationships

473. Empaths create the best when in their comfort zone

Empaths The Book

474. Empaths can get stuck in comfort zones that slow their growth

475. Empaths who worry about themselves and avoid getting pulled into drama win at life

476. Empaths feel for people in need

477. Empaths who find a passion for something put a lot of energy into it, making that thing come into fruition

478. Empaths may need time to relax and that's ok

479. Empaths should be more open with their friends and family about being an Empath for best results

480. Empaths who date Empaths have magical relationships

Empaths The Book

481. Empaths are awakening everyone on the planet to their true potential

482. Empaths are compassionate people

483. Empaths feel the flow but don't always go with it

484. Empaths know if they are going to be your friend for a long time when they meet you

485. Empaths who apply the law of attraction to their life win at life

486. Empaths are great inventors who sense upcoming trends in order to create new concepts

487. Empaths download information from the environment around them

488. Empaths will avoid people with bad intentions

Empaths The Book

489. Empath's intuition is not always right but it is very accurate

490. Empaths feel the energy of the world around them

491. Empaths are healers whose presence itself is healing

492. Empaths take on the emotional baggage of others

493. Empaths who find balanced friends win at life

494. Empaths have vision that if they chased they would catch

Empaths The Book

495. Empaths experience miraculous events with miraculous timing

496. Empaths love deeply and feel comforted when that love is returned

497. Empaths who keep a journal win at life

498. Empaths who listen to their intuition win at life

499. Empaths feel a miracle coming

500. Empaths are powerful beings once they realize who they are

501. Empaths detach from bad vibes to heal

502. Empaths heal by healing others

Empaths The Book

503. Empaths can feel when someone close to them is thinking about them

504. Empaths can feel when someone close to them is about to call

505. Empaths who practice a daily routine win at life

506. Empaths are not as accepted in mainstream society as they should be

507. Empaths pick up on patterns and seek to change them when those patterns lead to bad vibes or bad outcomes

508. Empaths love honestly

509. Empaths love genuine people

Guide Summary

This guide is made so that you may come back to it as needed. Read over each Empath sutra as often as you want to remind yourself or to learn more about yourself or other people who may be Empaths. Sometimes we forget who we are and need to be reminded so that we may stay on course with our life path. If this guide helped don't forget to become a patron of our online healing space on Patreon at patreon.com/themeditationfamily

Power to the Empaths!

Printed in Great Britain
by Amazon

74609413R00078